T0157513

Cancer Bites

and

I Bit Back

Tom Dmytriw

authorHOUSE

AuthorHouse™
1663 Liberty Drive
Bloomington, IN 47403
www.authorhouse.com
Phone: 833-262-8899

Published by AuthorHouse   08/24/2023

ISBN: 979-8-8230-1286-7 (sc)
ISBN: 979-8-8230-1285-0 (e)

Library of Congress Control Number: 2023914575

Print information available on the last page.

This book is printed on acid-free paper.

This ordeal was one hell of a journey and I want to extend my undying love and thanks to my dear wife, Gail, and my loving son, Nick, and of course, Maxie the wonder dog, whose love and caring was incalculable to my winning the battle.

I also want to thank my friends, pastor, and all of my caretakers, especially my dentist, who first found the lump on my throat which ultimately led to my recovery.

It is my wish that this book brings hope, advice, and a laugh, to those who are suffering from the Enemy….. remember, if I survived this nightmare, you will too!!!!

CONTENTS

CHAPTER 1

"TOM, YOU HAVE cancer." What a shitty way to start a day!

CHAPTER 2

THESE WERE THE words that my loving wife, Gail, told me as I was returning from work on a very, as it turns out, life-changing day for me.

My son, Nick, was sitting next to her in our living room with tears in his eyes as I was absolutely gob-smacked with, I am certain, a very ashen face!

My very clever response to this news was, "huh…………. really?"

This was certainly not the most alacritous thing to say, but in my defense, I was rather stunned as you would imagine I would be.

CHAPTER 3

LET ME START from the beginning when this sordid tale began.

First of all this will be a very unvarnished tale of my cancer battle from the onset, to the optimistic conclusion of this unexpected journey........as a background, I grew up in a very blue collar, rough town, where all boys played sports, chased girls, drank beer at an early age, etc., and my story will be told from that perspective; mix all of these ingredients together, and voila, my everyday language may be a bit salty to some, but I do have a rather "je ne sais quoi" aura about me that has certainly been a beneficial trait for me over the years.....in other words, I have gotten away with being weaselly over the years as I hope you will attest to.

This story is designed to show the pathos, and hopefully the humor, that my rather Heminwayesque journey took from the nadir to the zenith of this adventure.

You may be the judge of this at the end of the story!

With that in mind, I had just recently gone to my dentist for a routine check-up, and upon examining my neck, which I always thought was unusual, when he gave me a grave look with a furrowed brow and said, "Tom have you noticed this lump on your neck?"

Now, I had just had my annual physical a few weeks earlier and was given a clean bill of health by my mentally arthritic internist, but by the look my dentist had just given me, I got some butterflies in my stomach as my spider-sense started to tingle telling me that something was not kosher. He told me that I should make an appointment with my doctor as soon as possible.

As soon as I got home, I told Gail what the dentist had found.

As we all know, every family needs a mechanic, accountant, lawyer, etc., but the Dmytriw family has its own doctor, the eminent Dr. Gail, who immediately called up our doctor to schedule an appointment after her exam of my neck.

Now, since I had some dealing with fatty nodules over the years, and since the one in question was very small and almost invisible to the eye, I thought nothing of it but thank God, Gail reacted quickly, and made the appointment.

CHAPTER 4

MY APPOINTMENT WAS set for next week and with work traveling, household duties, etc., I did not give the lump much thought, but boy, I was always looking in the mirror and feeling the area to see if I could detect anything but in my new heightened, frightened state, this carbuncle seemed to be the size of a damned pumpkin!

When I saw our doctor, he had a very worried look on his face, and went out of his way to say that there was no way he would have missed this lump a few weeks back; he said this must have cropped up right after my recent physical. My thoughts on this can be summed up with one word, "BULLSHIT," you're just covering yourself......in my lifetime, I have come across some real cover your ass situations, but this one was a damned whopper....."this just happened"......sure it did.

WTF!!!!!

However, in the interests of decorum, I shut the hell up and listened to his blathering.

Well, I guess to cover his rather torpid previous physical with me, he gave me a REAL physical worthy of Dr. McCoy from Star Trek, minus his tricorder, of course, as I learned my odyssey of going to cancer specialists had just launched......starting with an ear, nose and throat specialist.

Outside of some childhood health issues, I had not been to a specialist in eons, and now my time in the wringer was just starting!

My poor wife has been encumbered with so many health problems, including surgeries, that I cannot even begin to list them; despite all she has gone through she has remained a trenchant lifestyle full of alacrity.

Funny thing is, during a tough time, or two, she would wax poetic about her problems and being a burden to us and I would tell her, in all sincerity, that the tables will be turning someday and it will be time in this cauldron of grief.....who knew I was going to be so prescient!

CHAPTER 5

THE TORTURE BEGINS!
My initial visit with the ENT specialist did not go well; I was nervous as hell and he was as cold as could be; shit, he reminded me of Mr. Freeze from the Batman comics. After his examination he stated that I would need a CT, and if things did not come back normal, I would need a surgical procedure to see what was going on.

He was so cold-hearted, and I was struck with so much fear, that I was pretty much tongue-tied, which I guess was a good thing because I had some rather colorful metaphors to acquaint him with due to the "warmth and comfort" he was showing.

Shit.

My first CT was scheduled, and I was very scared and nervous that I would make an ass out of myself showing my fear when the time came.

To most, this is a rather easy 1-2-3 procedure, but to me, it was devastating. You see, since being a child, I have a condition which is rather unusual and I guess, is part of the broad umbrella of being claustrophobic; we're not talking about some innate fear, but a full-fledged phobia that has manifested itself in many a nightmare over my life.

Damn, what a dilemma......and as it turned out, the subsequent treatments would only be worse as I went further down the rabbit hole of oncology.

Let me elaborate; I am not scared of enclosed places, as long as I am standing....when I am lying down on my back, with my arms not being able to move, I go ballistic and the same thing happens if I am wearing a tight sweater and can't get it off; this phobia really fucked me up when we were wrestling in high school PE classes, football practices, etc............UGH!!!!

I have traced this condition back to when I was five years old when I was getting a tonsillectomy back in New Jersey.

Hell, I can still remember this whole ordeal to this day............ every horrible moment of what I was feeling and remembering every single detail of what I went through .... let me pontificate.

Way back in the Stone Age, parents were not allowed to accompany their children up to the OR. I remember being downstairs in the hospital waiting room with my folks, who were doing their best to assuage me of the fear I was feeling, when the nurse came down, and it was time to go up for something that would eventually affect the rest of my life.

Sort of like livestock coming in from the fields, I was shepherded into a large "holding pen" with about ten kids who were already there playing with the various toys and other distractions available to get our minds off our impending surgeries.

Good God, even at the age of five, I was prescient enough to see what was going on.........how stupid did these grown-ups think we were???

Like a waiter grabbing a lobster from a restaurant's tank, a nurse would periodically come in and grab one of the uninformed, or vaporous children, and whisked them away into the great abyss.

After a while, as the amount of lobsters began to dwindle, I realized I was the last one left....so help me God, I was the last one.

By this time, I was feeling nervous, and missing my folks, when one of the Angels of Mercy came into the room and with a rather saccharine voice said, "please come with me."

Well, the shitshow that warped me for the rest of my life (more on this later), until recently, had just begun as I was unceremoniously placed on a metal chair outside of the OR I was soon to be in......can you believe that to put a five year old child unattended, on a metal chair outside the OR was the hospital's protocol???

Fuck this hospital!!

I sat there, alone, seemingly for hours until they came to get me and march me to the gallows where I still, to this day, vividly remember the anesthesiologist's mask being put on me as I PLEADED the doctors to stop.....I still remember my telling the surgeon, "please, please, please, stop," as he mask was being put on my face.

Unfortunately, to this day, these memories have never left me.

So you can see why I was absolutely catatonic when my doctors were telling me of Petscans, CT's, MRI's, and other tortures I would be going through during the cancer testing since every one of them involved the techniques that have so tortured me for so many years.

Damn, I had avoided any type of anesthesia for sixty years............hell, I don't even get the traditional colonoscopy because of this.

It's a damned phobia......what can I do??????????

Back to the present, just my luck, the CT came back and they were more ably to see what it was but they did not know exactly where it was yet. Initially, we were told it was not a tumor and I started doing handstands with this news............but wait just a minute my friends, the mass that was there would require a procedure, under GENERAL anesthesia, no less, to further investigate what was going on.

My face must have looked as if I had seen Bigfoot!

I was devastated and broke out in a cold sweat with just the thought of going through an operation and thinking how I would react with my phobia.

Dr. Gail drove home, and I don't think I said a word as I simply went to the love seat in our family room and hunkered down.....it was my only defense!

Thank God for my family and our beloved West Highland Terrier, Max.

To make matters worse, before the procedure I had to get a Petscan which really scared the shit out of me, because like a new toothbrush, I was going to be put inside a "tube" after first getting an IV that had radiation in it. My God when I saw the giant maw

I was going to be placed in, I thought I was being chased by a hungry T-Rex from Jurassic Park!

Being a comic book and avid sci-fi fan, I wondered if I was going to come out of the scan with supernatural powers; was I destined to become "Radiation Man" or some other comic book name like "Captain Cancer".....how can this be happening to me???

The day of this latest torture came and my technician was very kind-hearted as he saw my intense apprehension and tried to joke around with me, God bless him!

He explained everything in detail to me, and seeing that I still had a somewhat sense of humor, tried to joke around with me to temper my anxieties.

My primary doctor had given me some sedatives to take the edge off, and my technician said now is the time and we will come back for you in about half an hour.

The pill worked, to some degree, and when the time came, I walked a little gingerly, with assistance, of course, and got onto the gurney, trying to put on a brave face.

As I was being positioned into the tunnel, I told myself that this is no worse than going into a tanning bed from years past and continued to invoke help from God.

However, I could not help but be reminded by the scene at the end of Jaws when the captain of the boat was sliding down into the sharks gaping, razor-toothed giant mouth screaming in unbridled fear and terror......ugh!!

Happily, that was not the case with me and surprisingly I was calm enough that the testing did not overtly bother me, and it was time to go home and wait, AGAIN, for the results.

The results showed what the CT had, which was really good news, since there was absolutely no spread of the mass that was uncovered…..thank God!!

However, the next step was what I was told may be lurking…………the dreaded procedure that required GENERAL anesthesia.

Waiting for the day of the procedure was nothing short of tortuous, and I simply sat on the love seat in our rec room in a fetal position counting down the days, hours, and minutes until the Day of Reckoning came up.

I was having trouble sleeping already due to my nerves and fear of the unknown, but there is NOTHING WORSE THAN LATE-NITE CABLE TV because seemingly EVERY fucking commercial is about some form of cancer or other terminal disease which is something I really did not need to see, you know??

My God, I never knew there were so many horrible diseases out there and the miracle cures that can help you!

So, my sleep got worse and worse and I was not eating, so I was one sad sack of a person lying on the love seat…………..in the meantime, the clock was tick, tick, ticking away as the day of the procedure was rapidly coming into sight.

I was watching the clock so much that I was becoming myopic!

Procedure day came and while driving up to the hospital I felt like I was in an old western movie where some poor s.o.b. was about to be hanged.

As my wife dropped me off, the surgical employee who met me upon leaving the car turned out to be one of my friends who I had met at the local Irish music jams I attended on Saturday's over the years……..I was very surprised to see her, and after we bs'd a little bit while my wife parked the car, she said that she would stop by to see me before the procedure and told me not to worry since my surgeon was one of the best in the region.

Somewhat assuaged of a small portion of my anxiety, I still was in this surreal situation and I don't remember much about checking in, but I certainly felt as if the Sword of Damocles was ready to drop on my neck..........thank God for Gail being there to assist!

Eerily similar to my one and only procedure some 60 years ago, I went into my "stall" to await my turn in the torture chamber, when I was told that my doctor had to attend to an emergency which pushed back my operation around two hours............. Shades of Nicodemus!!!!

At this time, my friend had time to stop by to chat, and comfort me, since it did not take a professional to realize I was rather distraught, to put it mildly! She proved to be a real angel of mercy and was able to stay by me for quite some time.

Finally, my surgeon came in and told me we would be starting in a few minutes; to his credit, he tried to talk football to me to calm me down, but it had no effect on me, especially since I didn't like his Mr. Freeze cold demeanor that he first exhibited to me.

One of the nurses came to my stall and I trudged along to the OR; talk about a dead man walking,.......yikes, what a feeling!

I mustered up what courage I could, got onto the table, and before I knew it, I had woken up and was being helped to one of the waiting rooms.................Dr. Gail was absolutely correct that when I woke up, it would seem like a matter of seconds!

Upon waking up it did seem like just a few seconds had gone by, and I was escorted into one of the post-op rooms to wait until I was deemed okay to leave.

Dr. Gail came in and I felt really, really proud of myself that I had weathered this storm!

Well, we had to wait for the results to come in, which seemed endless, of course, and sure enough, as I had first mentioned to Gail that I thought this surgery would lead to others, as seemingly EVERY procedure pans out, we were indeed told a SECOND one was needed as I had adroitly predicted.

Dammit..........I had enough anxiety going through the first one, so my mind thought the worse and I started to freak out about going through this shit again.

Why the hell wasn't it all taken care of the first time??? Man, this wasn't kosher as the cosmic dice seemed to keep coming up snake eyes on me!

The only positive thing is that now that I had somewhat conquered the fear of the unknown, regarding my going through surgery and general anesthesia, I was not quite as frozen with fear as this phobia has rendered me in the past.

I thanked God for this miraculous event and let me tell you, the timing of my getting somewhat over this phobia was indeed fortuitous, as future treatments loomed.

But, I will say, that upon first hearing this news, I swore a tapestry of the foulest verbiage one can think of, which I believe is still hovering over our neighborhood; you know, some artists use paints, plaster, marble, etc., as their raw materials, but my medium, when provoked, is the delicious decadence of profanity which is my true medium at certain times!

The day of the second procedure came and this time, I was not very nervous at all and actually joked with my surgeon when we spoke in the pre-op room; he was certainly glad that my demeanor was not as anxious and combative as it was the first time.

In fact, if you can believe it, after they administered the anesthetic IV to me, unlike the first time, I actually awoke as the anesthesiologist was putting on my mask..............my God, if this had happened during my first procedure I would have stroked out for sure!

Shades of a million years ago when the mask was being put on me for my tonsillectomy; however, this time I looked at him and calmly said, "you didn't you use a mask last time," to which he answered, "yeah, I did, but you didn't realize it."

Seemingly seconds later, I awoke.

CHAPTER 6

MAY 17TH IS when my life changed.

So as I had stated in the beginning of this story, I had just come in from visiting some local customers for work, and Dr. Gail, Nicky, and Maxie were in our living room and they gave me the news which I didn't want to hear.............."Tom, you have cancer."

I have to admit, I was not completely surprised as I had started to come to the realization that there was at least a 50-50 chance of my having cancer, but there it was.

How the hell can I have cancer – I am never sick, I exercise, take vitamins, so naturally, I always thought I would live forever.

How in God's name do I cope with cancer, or the Enemy, as I called it.

Stay tuned my friends, for the answers!!!

As is my wont when something I receive is dyspeptic news, either physically, or emotionally, I went into my full-scale "internal attack mode" against the Enemy.........maybe my outward appearance showed the contrary, but believe me, I was extremely pissed that this fucking disease was now in my body and I was going to beat it!!!

It's like what a lot of sports fans do with the concept of negative luck......we pretend our team doesn't have a chance to win, when deep down inside we are expecting the opposite to happen.

Now, despite my liking to use "salty" language, mainly due to my years of playing sports, I have always been very religious and was never afraid to ask God for forgiveness, or other requests such as healing, and since I had always thought that this day would never rear its ugly head, I had always had plans to use my faith to fend off this inured situation if it ever arose.

Despite this vow, I have to admit that upon hearing, and fully comprehending this catastrophic news, I did harbor some very negative feelings as I was swamped with regrets castigating myself for past transgressions which make it difficult for me, at times, to live in the present with the ghosts of past sins haunting, and gnawing away at me.....surprisingly, these thoughts started to wane away as I forged ahead with the battle.

Growing up and seeing so many movies, TV shows, commercials, etc., regarding the "Big C," I had always thought, in the back of my mind, that if I ever contacted it, I would be VERY aggressive in combating it with my Faith..........well, that time had come.

During this rather inchoate time, I started searching the internet to find some comforting cancer-related prayers, message boards, etc., that proved to be a very healing balm for me.

Boy, this turned out to be the best thing I ever did!

I also started a daily "cancer diary" where I was able to jot down my thoughts and worries which I found to be VERY therapeutic!

CHAPTER 7

S O, MY CANCER life morphed into the healing/combatic stage.

Having played sports for many years, with some notoriety I may add, I can be very quietly aggressive when it comes to winning; sort of like the negative luck I just spoke about............ believe me, I never played in a game that I did not think we were going to win, or that I would be the hero, so deep inside I was seething at the Enemy and I certainly had NO intention of losing this battle!!

I now had to go to an oncologist and meet my radiation doctor; this entirely surreal experience became ever more hallucinogenic to me!

My oncologist turned out to be very energetic and upbeat; what a relief! He told me his father had a similar cancer years ago and that he recovered very nicely.

As was the case with all my doctors, he did a very thorough job of explaining what was in store for me from his side of things..........the dreaded CHEMOTHERAPY!!!!

I knew this was coming, so I wasn't blindsided at all by this news..............in fact, his soothing manner assuaged me of many of the apprehensions I was feeling and I was actually somewhat glad that we were attacking the Enemy so aggressively.

He mentioned that the chemo I was getting was a milder dosage due to what they had found during my procedure and that before I was administered the dosage to fight the cancer, I would first be given a dose of anti-nausea medicine to fend off any nefarious side effects I might get.

We spoke about side effects that I could expect going forward, yada-yada-yada, and, as just mentioned, he did an excellent job of succinctly going over what I could expect to deal with during these treatments....he did not sugarcoat anything, but his upbeat optimism was certainly a refreshing tonic for me to hear.....much better than what Dr. Sourpuss had initially told me!

He told me that I would be getting one treatment a week for a duration of six weeks, with each treatment lasting approximately four hours.........damn, what next??

All in all, not the best news, but not the worst...........reminded me of the old adage of, "besides that Mrs. Lincoln, how was the play?"

Leaving there, feeling great, Dr. Gail and I went to my radiation treatment consult which, in my naivete, I thought would be a walk in the park.........as it turned out, it was more akin to dodging landmines and was going to lead me down a road that I would not wish upon my worst enemy.

You know, there is an old saying that the cure is worse than the disease, and man was I going to be living proof of this!

As I have mentioned, this was during the height of the covid scare, so I found it unnerving to seeing so many folks in the waiting room wearing masks, carrying oxygen, and looking like the cast from Night of the Living Dead................ugh!!!!!!!!!!

To me this was akin to awaiting the abattoir to come and get me; sure enough, it was my time for the initial consult so Dr. Gail and I trudged into one of the examination rooms.

Once in the room, the nurse showed us a video of how the radiation treatment is administered. They had to make a personal "goalie's" face mask for me which I had to wear while I was being zapped with the radiation in another tube like enclosure........... when I saw what I had to go through for 35 sessions, I thought there was no way in hell I could go through this.

My radiation doctor was very young, and EXTREMELY somber, which like my EN&T doctor, minus the age, unnerved me mightily......I wanted to hear encouraging words........my God, I am a neophyte at having illnesses and I want to hear encouraging words!!

He gave me an extremely thorough explanation of what I could expect, the healing process, etc., and my mind was overwhelmed............thank God Dr. Gail was there.

After all of the horrible scenarios we were going through, I remember asking him pointblank, "is this curable?"

Again, very somberly, I guess due to the fact that he did not want to get my hopes up too high with promises of a cure, he assuaged me by nodding his head affirmatively and saying one word – "yes."

Turns out that my cancer, which was finally diagnosed at being on the back on my tongue is very, very common and has a high rate of being cured; the great thing was that my dentist had found the lump on my throat so early before there was any chance of this possibly metastasizing elsewhere.

Despite these encouraging words, by the time I got home, my head was spinning as if I had been drinking Jack and Coke all day!

Shit, at this this time I thought I was in some sort of bizarro Twelve Days of Christmas scenario as I had already gone through two CT's, two Petscans, two surgical procedures, an outside biopsy, a MRI, and a partridge in a pear tree.

And now I had weeks of radiation and chemo treatments that would be done concomitantly.....is it time to wake up yet from this fucking nightmare?

Man, I felt like a skier being overtaken by an avalanche, you know?

Upon hearing all of this recent catastrophic news, I enhanced my searches for cancer info and inspirational passages/videos that would help me fight back.

This strategy was one of the major ways I found to combat the Enemy.

CHAPTER 8

A S I WAS waiting for the chemo and radiation treatments to begin, I tried to stay positive that I would be cured of the Enemy.

In addition, I have always worked out, never smoked, watched my weight, did not drink much, as I tried to maintain a salubrious lifestyle.

So I figured that if I could keep this up and not morph into a querulous demeanor, this would help my winning the battle.

In trying to keep up my alacrity during these trials and fighting not to be saturnine, my first week of radiation and first chemo treatment was approaching rapidly which reminded me of prepping for finals during my college days, as I mentally psyched myself up for the ordeals to come.

As I waited at the radiation center the first day, Jim, a friend of ours from the Moose Lodge we belong to, who ironically had the exact same cancer as me, was walking out from the treatment center into the lobby, and as out eyes met, he smiled and said, "Tom, you got this, you are in great hands."

Jim was one of only about five people who knew what I was going through, and the way we found out that he had the same cancer was during a very fortuitous conversation we had at the Moose; we told him to please not to tell anyone, and he certainly upheld that request.

As it turns out, Jim was nearing the completion of his treatments and became a sort of "Sensei" for me as I began my journey..........for those who are not familiar with this word, when I took karate lessons this is what we called our instructor which in Korean translates to "one who gone on before" which is a great sign of respect.

So, I walked into the maelstrom ready for the fight of my life and in high benevolence for my being cured.

I mustered up my courage, and told the technicians, "let's get the healing started!"

I wore a tropical shirt, which all the technicians thought was great, got onto the "Rack" and closed my eyes and prayed mightily for God's healing to begin.

The mask did not trigger my phobia; I think in good part because I had totally prepped myself to deal with it such as getting ready for a big game many centuries ago in school.

I was told each treatment was 7-8 minutes long, and as I did with the various other scans I suffered through, I silently counted down the seconds and minutes and the next thing I knew, it was over and the techs said, "see you tomorrow."

I had survived round 1 of 35..........only 34 more treatments to go!!

UGH!!!!

A few days later was my chemo appointment; every Thursday, like the old Sunday doubleheaders that MLB had many moons ago, was my dual torture of radiation and "happy juice" which was my pet name for the stuff being coarsed through my veins.

The first thing with chemo is that you have to go into their prep area and get an IV; since they always had a problem with doing this for me, I looked like a pin cushion when I got home.

From there I was escorted into the chemo treatment room, and to say it was surreal is a massive understatement.

I looked around this massive room and all I saw were these large upright IV stands that reminded me of the scene from Jurassic Park when Dr. Grant and the kids were escaping the dinosaurs and took refuge in one of the giant trees when the brontosaurus heads started to pop up out of the jungle............shades of Salvadore Dali, or Picasso, how surreal was this??????????

It also reminded me, in a rather perverse way, of my mom going to the beauty parlor in the 60's and seeing an endless forest of hair dryers throughout the shop reaching to the heavens reminding me of the giant Redwoods that are found in California; also eerily reminiscent of the telescopic Martian warships from the classic sci-fi movie, War of the Worlds.......one of my all-time favorite movies!!!!

The first IV administered to me was the anti-nausea medicine where took about 45 minutes to drain into me; then came the "happy juice" for the next 3 ½ hours ..fantastic.

But I tell you, the treatment chairs were recliners with built-in heaters, I had internet and phone coverage, and enough outlets to make any internet junkie lick his chops; from an electronic geeks viewpoint this was like entering the world of Tron

Also, I was offered juices, candies, etc., so from a very obtuse point of view, it was like I was traveling first class in a jet or I was back on a Caribbean cruise; I naturally asked for a pina colada, which always got a laugh from the staff.

The nurses were first-class, and gave me fantastic service..........however, the thing that really disturbed me and got my knickers in a twist was seeing the poor souls who were really suffering from the serious life-threatening cancers they were afflicted with, and I felt a little guilty about my being bummed out over a cancer that I was told was 90% curable and would not have catastrophic side effects.

I felt embarrassed by my selfish thoughts!

CHAPTER 9

S O THE FIRST week of my wonderful summer season had begun.

From the beginning, Dr. Gail and I had made battle plans on how to defeat the Enemy and developed a strategy of staying mum about it, even to the majority of our friends and family.

As I previously mentioned, we did not tell anybody about my condition, except for a few who we knew we could trust not to gossip; it wasn't that we wanted to be surreptitious about this from our friends and family, but I didn't want people saying to me, "oh, what a shame; you know I had a relative who went trough this and they had some problems," yada, yada, yada.

NO, the last thing I wanted to hear was shit like this.

Additionally, since we had been told that my side effects would start to kick in around the halfway mark of my treatments, in about 3-4 weeks, we decided to continue to do things as we always did in the summer.....we are fortunate to belong to a country club with a GREAT pool, so we were definitely taking advantage of this as well as dining out and traveling.

I continued to wear tropical shirts to my treatments, "kibitzed" around with the technicians and tried to maintain a bright, confident countenance.

In the back of my mind, I kept telling myself that I felt fine and the upcoming side effects I was told to expect, would pass by.

Sounds terrific, right???

The best was yet to come!

CHAPTER 10

A S THE NEXT few weeks went by, sure enough, my taste started to go away and I was losing more and more weight.

At first, I thought this was kind of neat since I had been wanting to lose a few pounds and I was starting to develop a six-pack on my abdomen. However, along with the taste being seriously compromised, my appetite was waning incredibly, and I was starting to get sluggish. I was so sluggish that we stopped doing many of the activities we had been enjoying.

Almost like clockwork, during the fourth week of my treatments, I had dropped some twenty-five pounds and my doctors noticed this and raised their first alarms.

They sent me to a nutritionist, which did not work ....
does ANYONE like these liquid weight enhancers they push.............UGH!!!!!

So as I had reached the midpoint of my treatments, and what I was told to expect was now coming to fruition, I buckled up as I approached the finish line.

Little did I know the worst weeks of my life were on the horizon.

As the weight continued to fly off me at an alarming rate, I was now subjected with this non-stop coughing which produced a disgusting miasmic, gelatinous, phlegm-like substance, which I had to expectorate nearly every 5-10 minutes 24 hours a day...... good God, this was like hocking up raw oysters for 20 hours a day!

Dammit, I had trouble sleeping as it was, and now it was nearly impossible for me to do so because once I tried to sleep, the coughing would start and the phlegm would unceasingly continue until I expectorated into a cup that I now had at my side, as any rest that I may have needed, was compromised.

So, my brave front of wearing tropical shirts, kidding around, etc., came to a SCREECHING halt as I was now 30 pounds lighter.

In baseball parlance, when a team is out of the pennant race by the summer, and the games are meaningless with the weather being stifling hot, and there is seemingly no end to the mundane rest of the schedule, they are known as the "dog days," and sure enough this was how I was feeling.

In just a few weeks I turned 180 degrees from trying to be upbeat, to being completely dyspeptic as I continued to go through the laborious daily routine of radiation, plus my once a week baccalaureate of chemo giving me a heightened sensation of malaise.

As I said, although I was really in anguish both mentally and physically, the folks who administered my treatments were

FABULOUS, and thank God for them trying to keep my spirits up since I really getting into the depths of despair!

Now, once a week after a radiation treatment, I met with my doctor who gave me a quick exam to see how I was doing….in fact, he was quite pleased.

Well, on one particular shitty day he asked me how I was feeling and I responded, "just get a gun and kill me," which he took literally not knowing I was using a colorful metaphor to explain my thoughts at the moment.

My God, he was ashen-faced, and I thought for a moment the guys in the white coats were coming with the big net to drag me off to the loony bin!

Hello One Flew OVER the Cuckoo's Nest……..where's Jack Nicholson and Nurse Ratchet?????

After his realizing I was not suicidal, he calmed down and just told me to be patient regarding my taste and appetite.

So, the last few weeks of treatments followed and my metamorphosis into a complete enantiodromia person was almost finished.

As I approached my last days of treatments, I had lost approximately 50 pounds and still had little, to no, interest with eating.

Shit, this was not fair for a guy who loves to eat, and cook!

I cringed everytime I was weighed, since now they were really trying to talk me into getting a feeding tube, which was not going to happen.

I was so worried about getting weighed, that I actually started to wear sneakers and clothes that added some weight to my increasingly emaciated body. I was now living the classic Andy

Griffith Show episode when Barney, who had to be at a specific weight to keep his job, had a hiccupping spell prohibiting him from eating...........Andy, with his time-honored wisdom, put a concealed heavy chain around his neck, which was hidden from sight by his uniform shirt, helping him to reach the targeted weight since Andy realized that a deputy's dress code allowed for them to wear a chain, which is exactly what he and Barney adhered to.

If only that would have worked for me.

When my last chemo was done, they have a tradition for the patient to ring a bell signifying the end of this particular torture; being superstitious, I politely declined, took the certificate, said goodbye to the new friends I had made, and got ready for my last days of radiation.

So I bid adios to one of my major treatments and thanked God for helping me through this awful time better than I expected.

CHAPTER 11

A S POPEYE ALWAYS had his spinach to fall back on with his problems, I continued to use my faith to combat the Enemy.

By this time, we had told a few close friends about my condition, and sure enough, one of our closest friends who I had dubbed "Scoop" came to visit.

We called her Scoop since with her job she knows virtually everyone in our town and what is going on, as well. Scoop was my first visitor in six weeks, and since Dr. Gail had told her about my current "matinee idol" looks so she wasn't completely thunderstruck when she saw me.....I can't tell you how much I loathed taking a shower and looking in the mirror, since it reminded me of those poor emaciated souls you see on the History Channel's concentration camp documentaries.

My first words to her was a plea not to tell anyone how I looked, and of course, she listened to my piteous request.

Turns out that I had a nice, therapeutic time with her, which helped me to get through the day and get closer to the end of the radiation treatments.

Finally, the last day of my treatment came, and as I trudged towards the table, had my mask put on, and the radiation blanket draped over me, I started to ask God that when it was over, to please favor me with a clean bill of health and get me back to normal as quickly as possible.

Naturally, I had gotten very close to my technicians and they certainly were great with sympathizing over my distress, but one guy in particular was always right to the point.

I told him about my fear of the treatment being successful and my getting my taste back, and he said that he was certain that the cancer was gone and that in about two weeks I would start to get my appetite back.

I know he was no Karnak the Magnificent from Johnny Carson fame, but I certainly enjoyed hearing his encouraging words!

Just like that, through the grace of God, and my family, I had somehow navigated the fiercest storm I had ever faced.

As with my chemo acquaintances, I gave my thanks to everyone for being so helpful, and this time I did accept their certificate of completion of the treatments.

When I got home, as I had been doing for seven weeks, I again thanked God that I had made it through this ordeal and now it was in His hands as to whether the treatments had been successful.

As I sat on my couch, I started to think about what an ordeal this had been.........the surgeries, the endless scans, the chemo, the radiation, the loss of appetite and taste, special dental precautions to ensure that the radiation did not lead to any loss of teeth, etc., had all taken a tremendous toll on me, but you know what, there was some good that I encountered proving that there is such a thing as a cloud having a silver lining.

The most miraculous, inured circumstance that happened to me was my finally getting over the paranoia of my phobia for lying down with my hands unable to move freely; screw that lousy hospital from my childhood surgery.....I finally beat your memories that had been haunting me all of my life!

My relationship with God, which had always been excellent, was certainly strengthened exponentially by finding so many spiritual aids to help me during this time.

For example, I have never been a fan of those syndicated religious shows which I feel are full of bologna..........I mean come on, the phony phones ringing in the background of the "preacher" with their subliminal message of your opening your wallets to them; come on, what bullshit! Where is the FCC in stopping this nonsense?????

Man, we all need money, but how can these crooks rationalize playing on people's fears and trauma to extort their hard-earned money?

However, I did find one who is a legitimate preacher and his messages are done during his church services without the overt goal of extorting money from the poor souls who are so down on their luck that they would do anything to get healed.

In fact, I am hoping that I can do some motivational talks to cancer-stricken folks to let them know that if I went through this, they can also!!!

I had met so many nice individuals during this ordeal...........

even my ENT and radiation doctors became friends as I came to grips with the Enemy and my fear of the unknown started to wane.

Sure enough, just as my radiation technologist had told me, about two weeks into my recovery, I did start to feel a little more hungry and my taste improved.........I would say my taste was only about 40-50% from what it should be, but in my current world, that was astronomical.

It is hard to properly express my joy at starting to be able to eat foods again on a regular basis.........I continually thanked God for this happenstance!

My subsequent check-ups were all very positive and there were no signs of the Enemy anywhere; just to keep an eye on things, another Petscan was on the horizon, but by this time, I did not worry about this one iota............I can't believe I am writing these words now.

In fact, when I went for this Petscan it had now been several months since my treatments ended, so physically I was starting to gain back some of the 60 pounds I had lost, and my normal wise-ass personality was reemerging like the groundhog in Panxsutawney.

The Petscan tech and I had also bonded over the months, so as we were prepping for another dose of jungle juice to coarse through my veins, I quipped, "hey, is this scan free; I was thinking you might have a coupon deal here like buying so many subs until you get a free one!"

We both laughed heartily.

EPILOGUE

IT HAS NOW been going on two years since my last radiation treatment and I thank God for helping me have a speedy and successful recovery........... I am pretty much back to my normal, vivacious, handsome self – LOL – and I am looking forward for more improvements.

My cancer journey was indeed serpentine, full of ebbs and flows, with many rocks in the stream, but God saw me through this trial and He led me to forging an even stronger bond with Him through prayer and the many other resources that I found trudging through the wilderness...............Praise the Lord!!!!!!

In fact, this was the first prayer I had found on the internet back when the lump was discovered on my neck, which I think was one of the most relevant passages I have ever came across.

Loving God, I pray that you will comfort me in my suffering, lend skill to the hands of my healers, and bless the means used for my cure.

Give me such confidence in the power of your grace, that even when I am afraid, I may put my whole trust in you, through our Savior Jesus Christ, Amen.

This absolutely touches all the bases that concerned me............comfort, skill for my doctors and my treatments, and depending on God's grace to assuage me from my fears through Jesus.

Pretty powerful stuff, right???

As I mentioned previously, my daily routine of prayers and meditations were a huge part in my circumnavigating the procedures needed to defeat the Enemy.

Well, there is one thing I am always cognizant of........... cancer will be always be a part of my life; will it come back again, will it be worse, who knows?

I was left with several "souvenirs" from the Enemy, but I am EXTREMELY happy that my taste is back to nearly 100% and my appetite has returned to its normally ferocious self! I still have never fully recovered my singing voice (which many people may say is a good thing), and I still have a periodic nagging cough and dry mouth in the evening, but how can I complain when so many cancer patients who are in critical condition would do anything to be in my condition.

Very small paybacks for being cured of a disease that could have been much worse if not for my wonderful, sainted dentist who first noticed the lump in my neck.

None of us have any idea of the brevity or longevity of our

time on this Mortal Coil, but if I could survive the ordeals that I went through, with all my phobias and fears, I am hoping that for anyone going through similar travails, they may be able to get a smile out of my journey and take some solace from my story and understand how they can fight, and defeat, the Enemy.

I can't adequately express all of my love and thanks to my wonderful wife, son, Maxie the wonder dog, friends from church and elsewhere, my doctors and technicians, etc., that helped push a poor sad sack like myself over the finish line in the hardest race of my life......**THANKS TO ALL!!**

In conclusion, I may have had cancer, but as it turned out, I **DIDN'T** let it have me, and as per the title of this book, Cancer Bites and I Bit Back!!!!!!

Printed in the United States
by Baker & Taylor Publisher Services